Preface

About This Book

Mastering Angular

A Comprehensive Guide to Building Modern Web Applications

Angular is a powerful framework for building dynamic and responsive web applications. "Mastering Angular" is your ultimate resource for mastering this essential technology, whether you're a beginner or an experienced developer.

What You Will Learn:

- **Foundations of Angular:** Understand what Angular is, its key features, and how to set it up.

- **Building Components:** Learn how to create and use Angular components, the building blocks of any Angular application.

- **Data Binding and Services:** Explore the intricacies of data binding, dependency injection, and creating reusable services.

- **Routing and Navigation:** Master Angular's routing module to create single-page applications with smooth navigation.

- **Advanced Topics:** Dive into advanced concepts like reactive programming with RxJS, state management with NgRx, and optimizing performance.

- **Testing and Debugging:** Set up unit tests with Jasmine and Karma, and learn debugging techniques to ensure your applications are robust and error-free.

- **Deployment and Best Practices:** Learn best practices for deploying Angular applications and maintaining code quality.

Why This Book?

This book is uniquely crafted by artificial intelligence, ensuring up-to-date and comprehensive coverage of Angular. It distills complex concepts into clear, actionable insights, making it an invaluable guide for any developer seeking to build modern web applications.

Whether you're looking to streamline your development process, ensure consistent performance, or leverage the latest features of Angular, "Mastering Angular" provides the knowledge and tools you need to succeed.

Who Should Read This Book?

- **Front-End Developers:** Enhance your understanding of Angular to build dynamic and responsive web applications.

- **Full-Stack Developers:** Learn to integrate Angular with back-end technologies to create complete web solutions.

- **Web Application Developers:** Gain insights into advanced Angular techniques and best practices to optimize your projects.

Embark on your journey to mastering Angular today, and unlock the full potential of your web development projects.

1 Foundations of Angular

1.1 Introduction to Angular

Angular is a powerful and popular web application framework developed by Google. It provides developers with a comprehensive set of tools and features to build dynamic and responsive web applications. In this chapter, we will introduce you to the foundations of Angular and give you a solid understanding of its core concepts and principles.

1.1.1 What is Angular?

Angular is a TypeScript-based open-source framework that allows developers to build modern web applications. It follows the component-based architecture, where the application is divided into reusable and independent components. These components are responsible for rendering the user interface and handling user interactions.

Angular provides a rich set of features that make it easy to develop complex applications. It offers powerful data binding, dependency injection, and routing capabilities, among others. With Angular, you can create single-page applications (SPAs) that provide a seamless user experience by dynamically updating the content without refreshing the entire page.

1.1.2 Why Angular?

Angular has gained immense popularity among developers due to its robustness, scalability, and extensive tooling support. Here are some key reasons why you should consider using Angular for your web development projects:

1. **Modularity**: Angular promotes the use of modules, allowing you to organize your code into smaller, reusable

pieces. This modular approach makes it easier to maintain and test your application.

2. **Component-based architecture**: Angular's component-based architecture enables you to build complex user interfaces by composing smaller, reusable components. This approach promotes code reusability and separation of concerns.

3. **Powerful data binding**: Angular provides a powerful two-way data binding mechanism, which allows you to easily synchronize data between the model and the view. This simplifies the development process and reduces the amount of boilerplate code.

4. **Dependency injection**: Angular's dependency injection system makes it easy to manage dependencies between different parts of your application. This promotes code reusability, testability, and maintainability.

5. **Routing and navigation**: Angular's built-in routing module allows you to create navigation paths and handle the routing between different views in your application. This is essential for building SPAs with multiple pages.

6. **Extensive tooling support**: Angular has a rich ecosystem of tools and libraries that enhance the development experience. The Angular CLI (Command Line Interface) provides a set of powerful commands to scaffold, build, and test your Angular applications.

1.1.3 Getting Started with Angular

To start building Angular applications, you need to have a basic understanding of HTML, CSS, and JavaScript. Additionally, familiarity with TypeScript, a superset of JavaScript, is highly recommended as Angular is primarily written in TypeScript.

To set up your development environment, you will need to install Node.js and npm (Node Package Manager). Once installed, you can use npm to install the Angular CLI globally on your machine. The Angular CLI provides a command-line interface for creating and managing Angular projects.

With the Angular CLI installed, you can create a new Angular project by running the following command:

```
ng new my-app
```

This will create a new directory called *my-app* with a basic Angular project structure. You can navigate into the project directory and start the development server by running:

```
cd my-app
ng serve
```

This will start the development server and make your application available at *http://localhost:4200*. Any changes you make to your code will automatically trigger a rebuild and refresh the browser.

In the next sections, we will dive deeper into the architecture, components, modules, and services of Angular, giving you a solid foundation to build upon. Let's get started!

1.2 Angular Architecture

Angular is a powerful and flexible framework for building dynamic web applications. To fully understand and utilize Angular, it is essential to have a solid understanding of its architecture. In this section, we will explore the key components and concepts that make up the Angular architecture.

1.2.1 Introduction to Angular Architecture

At its core, Angular follows a component-based architecture. This means that the application is built by composing reusable and self-contained components. Each component encapsulates its own logic, data, and presentation, making it easier to develop, test, and maintain.

The architecture of an Angular application can be visualized as a tree-like structure, with the root component at the top and child components branching out from it. This hierarchical structure allows for the composition of complex user interfaces by combining smaller, reusable components.

1.2.2 Modules in Angular

Angular applications are organized into modules. A module is a logical grouping of related components, directives, services, and other artifacts. It acts as a container for these artifacts and provides a way to organize and manage them.

Modules help in keeping the application codebase modular and maintainable. They allow for better separation of concerns and enable lazy loading, which improves the application's performance by loading only the required modules when needed.

1.2.3 Components in Angular

Components are the building blocks of an Angular application. They are responsible for defining the user interface and behavior of a specific part of the application. Each component consists of a template, which defines the structure and layout of the component, and a class, which contains the component's logic and data.

Components can communicate with each other through inputs and outputs. Inputs allow data to flow into a component, while outputs emit events to notify parent components or other subscribers about changes or actions.

1.2.4 Services in Angular

Services in Angular are used to encapsulate and provide functionality that can be shared across multiple components. They are responsible for handling data retrieval, business logic, and other operations that are not directly related to the user interface.

Services are typically injected into components using dependency injection. This allows components to access and use the services without having to create instances of them manually. Dependency injection promotes loose coupling and makes the application more modular and testable.

1.2.5 Directives in Angular

Directives are another important part of the Angular architecture. They allow you to extend HTML with custom behavior and functionality. There are two types of directives in Angular: structural directives and attribute directives.

Structural directives, such as *ngIf* and *ngFor*, modify the structure of the DOM by adding or removing elements based on certain conditions. Attribute directives, on the other hand, modify the behavior or appearance of existing elements.

1.2.6 Dependency Injection in Angular

Dependency injection (DI) is a key concept in Angular. It is a design pattern that allows you to provide dependencies to a class or component from an external source. This makes the code more modular, reusable, and testable.

In Angular, DI is handled by the framework itself. You can define dependencies in the constructor of a class or component, and Angular will automatically resolve and provide the required dependencies when creating instances of the class or component.

1.2.7 Angular CLI

The Angular Command Line Interface (CLI) is a powerful tool that helps in scaffolding, building, and testing Angular applications. It provides a set of commands that automate common development tasks, such as creating components, generating modules, and running tests.

The Angular CLI also comes with built-in support for features like code linting, bundling, and optimizing the application for production deployment. It greatly simplifies the development workflow and allows developers to focus on writing code rather than configuring the build process.

In this section, we have explored the key components and concepts that make up the Angular architecture. Understanding the architecture is crucial for building scalable and maintainable Angular applications. In the next section, we will dive deeper into Angular components and learn how to create and use them effectively.

1.3 Angular Components

In Angular, components are the building blocks of a web application. They are responsible for defining the structure, behavior, and appearance of different parts of the user interface. Components encapsulate the logic and data associated with a specific part of the application, making it easier to manage and reuse code.

1.3.1 What are Components?

Components in Angular are self-contained entities that combine the HTML template, CSS styles, and TypeScript code into a single cohesive unit. Each component represents a specific part of the user interface, such as a header, sidebar, or form. By dividing the application into smaller components, developers can easily manage and maintain the codebase.

1.3.2 Anatomy of a Component

A typical Angular component consists of three main parts: the template, the class, and the metadata.

Template

The template defines the structure and layout of the component's view. It is written in HTML and may include Angular-specific syntax and directives. The template is responsible for rendering the data and interacting with the user.

Class

The class contains the TypeScript code that defines the component's behavior and data. It includes properties, methods, and lifecycle hooks. The class interacts with the template and handles user interactions, data manipulation, and communication with other components or services.

Metadata

The metadata is defined using a decorator, which is a special kind of declaration that modifies the behavior of the class. The decorator provides information about the component, such as its selector, template, styles, and dependencies. It allows Angular to understand and instantiate the component correctly.

1.3.3 Creating a Component

To create a component in Angular, you need to follow a few steps:

7. Generate the component using the Angular CLI or create the necessary files manually.

8. Define the component's selector, template, styles, and other metadata using the decorator.

9. Write the TypeScript code in the component class to handle the component's behavior and data.

10. Use the component in other parts of the application by referencing its selector in the HTML templates.

1.3.4 Component Communication

Components in Angular can communicate with each other using various techniques. The most common methods of communication include:

Input and Output Properties

Components can pass data to child components using input properties and receive data from child components using output properties. This allows for parent-child communication and enables the sharing of data between components.

Event Emitters

Components can emit events using event emitters. This allows child components to notify parent components about specific actions or changes. Event emitters enable bidirectional communication between components.

Services

Components can communicate with each other through services. Services are singleton objects that provide functionality and data to multiple components. They act as a central point of communication and data sharing between components.

1.3.5 Component Lifecycle Hooks

Angular provides a set of lifecycle hooks that allow developers to tap into different stages of a component's lifecycle. These hooks provide opportunities to perform actions at specific moments, such as initialization, change detection, and destruction. Some of the commonly used lifecycle hooks include:

ngOnInit

This hook is called after the component has been initialized and its inputs have been bound. It is commonly used to perform initialization tasks, such as retrieving data from a server or setting up subscriptions.

ngOnChanges

This hook is called whenever the component's input properties change. It allows the component to react to changes in its inputs and update its internal state accordingly.

ngOnDestroy

This hook is called just before the component is destroyed. It is used to clean up resources, such as unsubscribing from subscriptions or releasing memory.

1.3.6 Component Styling

Angular provides several ways to style components, including inline styles, external stylesheets, and component-specific styles. Developers can choose the approach that best suits their needs and preferences.

Inline Styles

Inline styles allow developers to define styles directly in the component's template using the $style$ attribute. This approach is useful for small, component-specific styles that do not need to be reused.

External Stylesheets

External stylesheets can be used to define styles in separate CSS files and then linked to the component. This approach allows for better organization and reuse of styles across multiple components.

Component-Specific Styles

Angular also supports component-specific styles, which are defined directly in the component's metadata using the $styles$ property. This approach keeps the styles closely tied to the component and avoids global style conflicts.

1.3.7 Conclusion

Components are the fundamental building blocks of an Angular application. They encapsulate the logic, structure, and appearance of different parts of the user interface. By dividing the application into smaller, reusable components, developers can create dynamic and responsive web applications with ease. In the next section, we will explore Angular modules, which provide a way to organize and manage components within an application.

1.4 Angular Modules

In Angular, modules play a crucial role in organizing and structuring your application. They provide a way to encapsulate related functionality, making it easier to manage and maintain your codebase. In this section, we will explore the concept of Angular modules and how they can be used to enhance the modularity and reusability of your application.

1.4.1 Introduction to Angular Modules

An Angular module is a container for a cohesive set of related components, directives, pipes, and services. It acts as a boundary that encapsulates the functionality and dependencies of a specific feature or section of your application. By organizing your code into modules, you can achieve better separation of concerns and improve the overall maintainability of your application.

Angular modules are defined using the *@NgModule* decorator. This decorator allows you to specify the components, directives, pipes, and services that belong to the module. Additionally, you can configure various aspects of the module, such as imports, exports, and providers.

1.4.2 Creating Angular Modules

To create a new Angular module, you can use the Angular CLI or manually create the necessary files. The Angular CLI provides a convenient way to generate a new module using the *ng generate module* command. This command will create a new module file with the necessary boilerplate code.

When creating a module manually, you need to create a new TypeScript file and import the *NgModule* decorator from *@angular/core*. You can then decorate the module class with the *@NgModule* decorator and configure its properties.

1.4.3 Configuring Angular Modules

When configuring an Angular module, there are several properties that you can specify:

- *declarations*: This property is used to specify the components, directives, and pipes that belong to the module. These are the elements that can be used within the module or exported to other modules.

- *imports*: This property is used to specify the modules that are required by the current module. You can import both Angular modules and third-party modules.

- *exports*: This property is used to specify the components, directives, and pipes that should be made available for other modules to use. By exporting certain elements, you can create a public API for your module.

- *providers*: This property is used to specify the services that are provided by the module. Services defined at the module level are shared across all components within the module.

- *bootstrap*: This property is used to specify the root component of the module. This component will be bootstrapped when the module is loaded.

1.4.4 Using Angular Modules

Once you have created and configured an Angular module, you can use it in your application by importing it into other modules. This allows you to leverage the functionality provided by the module and use its components, directives, pipes, and services.

To import a module, you need to add it to the *imports* array of the module that requires it. This will make the exported elements of the imported module available for use within the importing module.

Angular follows a hierarchical structure for modules, where modules can import other modules. This allows you to create a modular architecture for your application, with each module encapsulating a specific feature or functionality.

1.4.5 Lazy Loading Modules

Angular also supports lazy loading of modules, which can significantly improve the performance of your application. Lazy loading allows you to load modules on-demand, only when they are required. This can reduce the initial load time of your application and improve the overall user experience.

To enable lazy loading, you need to configure your routes to load the corresponding modules lazily. This can be done by using the *LoadChildren* property in the route configuration. When a route is accessed, Angular will dynamically load the corresponding module and render its components.

Lazy loading is particularly useful for large applications with multiple feature modules. By lazy loading modules, you can split your application into smaller chunks and load them only when needed, reducing the initial bundle size and improving performance.

1.4.6 Conclusion

Angular modules are a fundamental building block of Angular applications. They provide a way to organize and structure your code, making it more modular and maintainable. By creating and configuring modules, you can encapsulate related functionality and improve the reusability of your code. Additionally, lazy loading modules can enhance the performance of your application by loading modules on-demand. Understanding and effectively using Angular modules is essential for building dynamic web applications with Angular.

1.5 Angular Services

In Angular, services play a crucial role in building dynamic web applications. They are responsible for providing functionality that can be shared across multiple components, modules, or even the entire application. Services are used to encapsulate business logic, handle data retrieval and manipulation, and facilitate communication between different parts of the application.

1.5.1 Introduction to Angular Services

Angular services are a fundamental part of the Angular architecture. They are typically used to separate concerns and promote code reusability. Services are implemented as classes and can be injected into other components or services using Angular's dependency injection mechanism.

One of the key advantages of using services is that they allow for the separation of concerns between the presentation layer (components) and the business logic layer. By encapsulating complex logic within services, components can focus on rendering the user interface and responding to user interactions, while services handle the underlying data manipulation and communication with external APIs.

1.5.2 Creating Angular Services

To create an Angular service, you can use the *@Injectable* decorator provided by Angular. This decorator marks the class as a service and allows it to be injected into other components or services. Services can be generated using the Angular CLI command *ng generate service*.

Once a service is created, you can define methods and properties that provide the desired functionality. For example, a service might have methods for retrieving data from a server, performing calculations, or handling authentication. Services can also have properties that store state or configuration information.

1.5.3 Using Angular Services

To use a service in a component, you need to inject it into the component's constructor. Angular's dependency injection system takes care of creating an instance of the service and providing it to the component. This allows the component to access the service's methods and properties.

To inject a service, you need to specify it as a parameter in the component's constructor and mark it with the *private* or *public* access modifier. Angular will automatically resolve the dependencies and provide an instance of the service when the component is created.

Once a service is injected into a component, you can access its methods and properties using the injected instance. This allows you to leverage the functionality provided by the service within the component's logic and template.

1.5.4 Dependency Injection in Angular

Angular's dependency injection system is a powerful feature that simplifies the management of dependencies between different parts of an application. It allows you to define dependencies in a declarative manner and ensures that the correct instances are provided at runtime.

When a component or service has a dependency, it declares it as a parameter in its constructor. Angular's dependency injection system then resolves the dependencies by creating instances of the required services and injecting them into the constructor.

This approach has several benefits. It promotes loose coupling between components and services, making it easier to replace or modify dependencies without affecting other parts of the application. It also simplifies testing, as dependencies can be easily mocked or replaced with stub implementations.

1.5.5 Reusable Services

One of the key advantages of using services in Angular is their reusability. Services can be designed to provide a specific set of functionality that can be used across multiple components or modules.

By encapsulating common functionality within services, you can avoid code duplication and promote a modular and maintainable codebase. For example, you might have a service that handles authentication, another service that manages data retrieval from a server, and yet another service that performs calculations or transformations on data.

By separating these concerns into individual services, you can easily reuse them in different parts of your application. This not only improves code organization but also makes it easier to maintain and update the functionality provided by the services.

In conclusion, Angular services are a crucial part of building dynamic web applications. They allow for the separation of concerns, promote code reusability, and simplify the management of dependencies. By leveraging services effectively, you can create modular, maintainable, and scalable Angular applications.

2 Building Components

2.1 Creating Angular Components

In Angular, components are the building blocks of a web application. They encapsulate the logic and presentation of a specific part of the user interface, making it easier to manage and reuse code. In this section, we will explore how to create Angular components and understand their structure and functionality.

2.1.1 Component Structure

An Angular component consists of three main parts: the template, the class, and the metadata. The template defines the HTML markup and the presentation of the component. The class contains the logic and data for the component, while the metadata provides additional information about the component.

To create a new component, you can use the Angular CLI (Command Line Interface) or manually create the necessary files. The CLI provides a convenient way to generate the component files with a single command. Once the component files are created, you can start customizing them to suit your needs.

2.1.2 Component Metadata

The metadata for a component is defined using a decorator called @Component. This decorator is used to specify various properties of the component, such as the selector, template, styles, and more. The selector is a unique identifier for the component, which can be used to include the component in other parts of the application.

2.1.3 Component Class

The component class is where you define the logic and data for the component. It is written in TypeScript, a superset of JavaScript that adds static typing and other features. The class is responsible for handling user interactions, manipulating data, and communicating with other components or services.

Within the component class, you can define properties and methods that are used by the template or other parts of the application. You can also use lifecycle hooks, such as *ngOnInit*, to perform initialization tasks when the component is created.

2.1.4 Component Template

The template is an HTML file that defines the structure and layout of the component. It can include data bindings, event bindings, and other Angular directives to dynamically render content and respond to user interactions. The template can also include other components, allowing you to compose complex user interfaces from smaller, reusable parts.

Angular provides a powerful templating engine that supports features like interpolation, property binding, event binding, and structural directives. These features allow you to create dynamic and interactive user interfaces with ease.

2.1.5 Component Styling

Styling is an important aspect of web development, and Angular provides several options for styling components. You can use CSS stylesheets, inline styles, or even CSS frameworks like Bootstrap to style your components. Angular also supports component-specific styles, allowing you to encapsulate styles within a component and prevent them from affecting other parts of the application.

2.1.6 Component Interaction

Components can communicate with each other using input and output properties. Input properties allow data to flow into a component, while output properties emit events to notify parent components about changes or actions. This mechanism enables the creation of modular and reusable components that can be easily composed and combined to build complex applications.

2.1.7 Component Lifecycle

Angular provides a set of lifecycle hooks that allow you to perform actions at specific stages of a component's lifecycle. For example, the *ngOnInit* hook is called when the component is initialized, while the *ngOnDestroy* hook is called when the component is about to be destroyed. These hooks provide opportunities to perform initialization, cleanup, or other tasks as needed.

2.1.8 Summary

In this section, we explored the basics of creating Angular components. We learned about the component structure, metadata, class, template, styling, interaction, and lifecycle. Components are the building blocks of an Angular application, and understanding how to create and use them is essential for building dynamic and responsive web applications. In the next section, we will dive deeper into using Angular components and explore various techniques and best practices.

2.2 Using Angular Components

In the previous section, we learned how to create Angular components. Now, let's explore how to use these components effectively in our web applications. Angular components are the building blocks of our application's user interface, and understanding how to use them correctly is crucial for creating dynamic and responsive web applications.

2.2.1 Component Composition

One of the key features of Angular is its ability to compose components together to create complex user interfaces. In Angular, we can nest components inside other components, creating a hierarchical structure. This allows us to break down our application into smaller, reusable pieces, making it easier to manage and maintain.

To use a component within another component, we need to import the component class and add it to the *declarations* array of the module that will use it. Once imported, we can use the component's selector as a custom HTML element within the template of the parent component. This way, we can include the child component and pass data to it using input properties.

2.2.2 Input and Output Properties

Input and output properties are a powerful way to communicate between parent and child components. Input properties allow us to pass data from the parent component to the child component, while output properties enable the child component to emit events back to the parent component.

To define an input property, we use the *@Input* decorator in the child component class. This decorator allows us to bind a property of the child component to a property of the parent component. By doing so, we can pass data from the parent component to the child component.

On the other hand, to define an output property, we use the *@Output* decorator in the child component class. This decorator allows us to emit events from the child component to the parent component. By doing so, we can notify the parent component about certain actions or changes that occurred within the child component.

2.2.3 Component Lifecycle Hooks

Angular provides a set of lifecycle hooks that allow us to tap into different stages of a component's lifecycle. These hooks provide us with the ability to perform certain actions at specific moments, such as when a component is created, rendered, or destroyed.

Some of the commonly used lifecycle hooks include *ngOnInit*, *ngOnChanges*, *ngAfterViewInit*, and *ngOnDestroy*. These hooks enable us to perform tasks like initializing component properties, subscribing to observables, or cleaning up resources when a component is destroyed.

Understanding the component lifecycle hooks is essential for managing component state, performing initialization tasks, and optimizing performance.

2.2.4 Component Communication with Services

Components often need to communicate with services to fetch data, perform calculations, or share data between different components. Services act as a bridge between components and provide a way to share data and functionality across the application.

To use a service within a component, we need to inject it into the component's constructor using Angular's dependency injection mechanism. Once injected, we can access the service's methods and properties within the component.

By separating the business logic into services, we can achieve better code organization, reusability, and testability. Services can be shared across multiple components, ensuring that the application follows the DRY (Don't Repeat Yourself) principle.

2.2.5 Component Styling

Styling is an essential aspect of web development, and Angular provides various ways to style components. We can use CSS stylesheets, inline styles, or even apply styles programmatically using Angular's style binding syntax.

By default, Angular encapsulates component styles, ensuring that they don't interfere with other components or the global styles of the application. This encapsulation is achieved by adding unique attributes to the component's HTML elements, creating a scoped CSS environment.

In addition to traditional CSS, Angular also supports pre-processors like Sass or Less, allowing us to write more maintainable and modular stylesheets.

2.2.6 Conclusion

In this section, we explored how to use Angular components effectively. We learned about component composition, input and output properties, component lifecycle hooks, component communication with services, and component styling. Understanding these concepts is crucial for building dynamic and responsive web applications with Angular. In the next section, we will dive deeper into styling Angular components and explore advanced styling techniques.

2.3 Styling Angular Components

Styling is an essential aspect of building web applications. In Angular, styling components is a breeze thanks to its powerful and flexible styling capabilities. In this section, we will explore various techniques and best practices for styling Angular components.

2.3.1 Inline Styles

One way to style Angular components is by using inline styles. Inline styles allow you to define styles directly within the component's template using the *style* attribute. This approach is useful for applying simple styles to individual elements.

To apply inline styles, you can use the *style* attribute followed by CSS property-value pairs. For example:

```
<div style="color: red; font-size: 16px;">Hello, Angular!</
div>
```

In the above example, the *div* element will have red text color and a font size of 16 pixels.

While inline styles are convenient for quick styling, they can become cumbersome when dealing with complex styles or applying styles to multiple elements. In such cases, it is recommended to use other styling techniques.

2.3.2 CSS Classes

CSS classes provide a more organized and reusable way to style Angular components. By defining CSS classes, you can apply styles to multiple elements and easily modify them in one place.

To use CSS classes in Angular components, you can leverage the *class* attribute in the component's template. You can bind the *class* attribute to a property in the component's class and dynamically apply or remove CSS classes based on certain conditions.

```
<div [class.myClass]="condition">Hello, Angular!</div>
```

In the above example, the *myClass* CSS class will be applied to the *div* element when the *condition* property in the component's class evaluates to true.

You can also apply multiple CSS classes by binding to an array of class names:

```
<div [class]="['class1', 'class2']">Hello, Angular!</div>
```

In this case, both *class1* and *class2* will be applied to the *div* element.

2.3.3 Component Stylesheets

Angular provides the ability to define component-specific stylesheets. These stylesheets are scoped to the component and do not affect other components or elements in the application.

To create a component stylesheet, you can use the *styleUrls* property in the component's metadata. This property accepts an array of stylesheet URLs that will be loaded and applied to the component.

```
@Component({
  selector: 'app-my-component',
  templateUrl: './my-component.component.html',
  styleUrls: ['./my-component.component.css']
})
```

In the above example, the *my-component.component.css* stylesheet will be applied to the *app-my-component* component.

Component stylesheets follow the same syntax as regular CSS files, allowing you to define styles for the component's template. You can use CSS selectors to target specific elements within the component and apply styles accordingly.

2.3.4 CSS Preprocessors

If you prefer using CSS preprocessors like Sass or Less, Angular has built-in support for them. Preprocessors offer additional features such as variables, mixins, and nesting, which can greatly enhance your styling workflow.

To use a CSS preprocessor in Angular, you need to install the corresponding preprocessor package and configure the build system accordingly. Once set up, you can write your stylesheets using the preprocessor syntax, and Angular will compile them into regular CSS during the build process.

2.3.5 CSS Framework Integration

Angular seamlessly integrates with popular CSS frameworks like Bootstrap, Material Design, and Tailwind CSS. These frameworks provide a set of pre-defined styles and components that you can leverage to quickly build visually appealing and responsive web applications.

To integrate a CSS framework into your Angular project, you can either include the framework's CSS files directly in your project or use a package manager like npm to install the framework as a dependency. Once integrated, you can use the framework's classes and components in your Angular templates.

2.3.6 Theming

Theming is an important aspect of styling Angular applications. It allows you to define a consistent visual style across your application and easily switch between different themes.

Angular Material, a popular UI component library for Angular, provides a theming system that allows you to customize the appearance of your application. You can define your own color palettes, typography styles, and other theme-related properties.

To apply a theme in Angular Material, you can use the *@import* statement in your component's stylesheet to import the desired theme file. Once imported, you can use the theme's classes and styles in your templates.

2.3.7 Best Practices

When styling Angular components, it is important to follow best practices to ensure maintainability and scalability of your codebase. Here are some best practices to consider:

- Use component-specific stylesheets whenever possible to keep styles isolated and avoid conflicts.

- Leverage CSS classes and CSS preprocessors to create reusable styles and improve code organization.

- Follow a consistent naming convention for CSS classes and selectors to make your styles more readable and maintainable.

- Use a CSS framework or UI component library to speed up development and ensure a consistent visual style.

- Consider using a theming system to easily switch between different visual styles and customize your application's appearance.

By following these best practices, you can create well-structured and maintainable styles for your Angular components.

In this section, we explored various techniques for styling Angular components, including inline styles, CSS classes, component stylesheets, CSS preprocessors, CSS framework integration, theming, and best practices. With these tools and practices at your disposal, you can create visually appealing and responsive web applications using Angular.

3 Data Binding and Services

3.1 Introduction to Data Binding

Data binding is a fundamental concept in Angular that allows you to establish a connection between the data in your application and the user interface. It enables you to effortlessly synchronize data between the model and the view, ensuring that any changes made in one are automatically reflected in the other. This powerful feature eliminates the need for manual manipulation of the DOM, making your code more concise and maintainable.

In Angular, there are four types of data binding: interpolation, property binding, event binding, and two-way binding. Each type serves a specific purpose and provides a different way to interact with your application's data.

3.1.1 Interpolation

Interpolation is the simplest form of data binding in Angular. It allows you to embed expressions within double curly braces ({{ }}) directly in your HTML templates. These expressions are evaluated by Angular and the result is displayed in the corresponding location in the view.

For example, suppose you have a component with a property called *name* that holds the value "John". By using interpolation, you can display the value of *name* in your template as follows:

```
<p>Welcome, {{ name }}!</p>
```

When the template is rendered, Angular will replace {{ name }} with the value of the *name* property, resulting in the following output:

```
Welcome, John!
```

Interpolation is a one-way binding, meaning that changes to the property in the component will not be reflected in the view automatically. To achieve two-way binding, you can use the *ngModel* directive, which we will explore in the next section.

3.1.2 Property Binding

Property binding allows you to set the value of an HTML element's property or attribute based on a property in your component. It is denoted by square brackets (*[ ]*) and can be used to bind to both standard HTML properties and custom component properties.

To illustrate, let's say you have a component with a property called *imageUrl* that holds the URL of an image. You can bind this property to the *src* attribute of an *<img>* element as follows:

```
<img [src]="imageUrl" alt="Image">
```

In this example, the value of the *imageUrl* property will be dynamically assigned to the *src* attribute of the *<img>* element. If the value of *imageUrl* changes in the component, the *src* attribute will be updated accordingly.

Property binding is a one-way binding, meaning that changes to the property in the component will be reflected in the view, but not vice versa.

3.1.3 Event Binding

Event binding allows you to respond to user interactions, such as button clicks or form submissions, by executing methods in your component. It is denoted by parentheses (*( )*) and can be used to bind to both standard HTML events and custom component events.

For example, suppose you have a button in your template and you want to call a method called *onClick* in your component when the button is clicked. You can achieve this by using event binding as follows:

```
<button (click)="onClick()">Click me</button>
```

In this example, the *click* event of the button is bound to the *onClick* method in the component. When the button is clicked, Angular will execute the *onClick* method.

Event binding is a one-way binding, meaning that it only triggers the execution of a method in the component. It does not update any properties or values in the view.

3.1.4 Two-Way Binding

Two-way binding is a powerful feature in Angular that allows you to establish a bidirectional connection between a property in your component and an input field in your template. It combines both property binding and event binding into a single syntax, using the *ngModel* directive.

To demonstrate, let's say you have an input field in your template and you want to bind its value to a property called *username* in your component. You can achieve this by using two-way binding as follows:

```
<input [(ngModel)]="username" type="text">
```

In this example, the value of the *username* property will be synchronized with the value of the input field. Any changes made to the input field will update the *username* property, and any changes made to the *username* property will update the input field.

Two-way binding provides a convenient way to handle user input and keep your component and template in sync.

3.1.5 Conclusion

Data binding is a crucial aspect of building dynamic web applications with Angular. It allows you to effortlessly synchronize data between the model and the view, providing a seamless user experience. In this section, we explored the different types of data binding in Angular, including interpolation, property binding, event binding, and two-way binding. Understanding and effectively utilizing data binding will greatly enhance your ability to create responsive and interactive applications.

3.2 Two-Way Data Binding

In Angular, data binding is a powerful feature that allows you to establish a connection between the data in your application and the user interface. It enables you to keep the data and the UI in sync, ensuring that any changes made to the data are immediately reflected in the UI, and vice versa. One of the most commonly used types of data binding in Angular is two-way data binding.

3.2.1 Understanding Two-Way Data Binding

Two-way data binding is a mechanism that allows you to bind a property of a component to an input element in the template, so that changes in either the component or the input element are automatically propagated to the other. This means that when the user interacts with the input element, the component's property is updated, and when the component's property changes, the input element is updated accordingly.

To implement two-way data binding in Angular, you can use the *[(ngModel)]* directive. This directive combines the property binding syntax *[property]="value"* and the event binding syntax *(event)="handler()"* into a single statement, making it easy to establish a two-way binding between a component property and an input element.

3.2.2 Using Two-Way Data Binding

To demonstrate how two-way data binding works, let's consider a simple example. Suppose you have a component that represents a user profile, and you want to allow the user to edit their name. You can achieve this by using two-way data binding.

First, you need to import the *FormsModule* from *@angular/forms* in your module file to enable the use of the *ngModel* directive. Then, in your component's template, you can bind the *name* property of the component to an input element using the *[(ngModel)]* directive:

```
<input [(ngModel)]="name" type="text">
```

In the above code, the *name* property of the component is bound to the value of the input element. Any changes made to the input element will automatically update the *name* property of the component, and any changes made to the *name* property will be reflected in the input element.

3.2.3 Handling Two-Way Data Binding

When using two-way data binding, Angular automatically generates an event named *ngModelChange* for each property that is bound using *[(ngModel)]*. This event is emitted whenever the value of the property changes.

You can handle this event by defining a method in your component and binding it to the *ngModelChange* event using the event binding syntax. For example, if you want to perform some validation or additional logic when the *name* property changes, you can define a method in your component and bind it to the *ngModelChange* event:

```
<input [(ngModel)]="name" (ngModelChange)="onNameChange($ev
ent)" type="text">
```

In the above code, the *onNameChange* method is called whenever the value of the input element changes. The new value of the input element is passed as an argument to the method, which you can then use to perform any necessary logic.

3.2.4 Limitations of Two-Way Data Binding

While two-way data binding is a powerful feature, it's important to use it judiciously and be aware of its limitations. One limitation is that it can make your code more complex and harder to understand, especially when dealing with complex data structures or multiple levels of nesting.

Another limitation is that two-way data binding can have performance implications, especially when used with large datasets or in scenarios where frequent updates are expected. In such cases, it's recommended to consider alternative approaches, such as using one-way data binding or implementing custom change detection strategies.

3.2.5 Summary

Two-way data binding is a powerful feature in Angular that allows you to establish a connection between a component property and an input element in the template. It enables you to keep the data and the UI in sync, ensuring that any changes made to the data are immediately reflected in the UI, and vice versa.

To use two-way data binding, you can use the *[(ngModel)]* directive, which combines property binding and event binding into a single statement. You can handle the changes to the property by defining a method and binding it to the *ngModelChange* event.

However, it's important to use two-way data binding judiciously and be aware of its limitations. It can make your code more complex and harder to understand, and it can have performance implications in certain scenarios. It's recommended to consider alternative approaches when dealing with complex data structures or performance-sensitive scenarios.

3.3 Dependency Injection

In this section, we will explore the concept of dependency injection (DI) in Angular. Dependency injection is a design pattern that allows us to create loosely coupled components by providing the dependencies they require from an external source. This approach promotes modularity, reusability, and testability in our codebase.

3.3.1 Understanding Dependency Injection

Dependency injection is a fundamental concept in Angular that enables us to manage the dependencies of our components. Instead of creating dependencies within the component itself, we can declare them as constructor parameters and let Angular handle the instantiation and injection of these dependencies.

By using dependency injection, we can easily swap out dependencies, mock them for testing purposes, and decouple our components from the specific implementation details of their dependencies. This makes our code more flexible, maintainable, and easier to test.

3.3.2 Injecting Dependencies

In Angular, we can inject dependencies into our components, services, and other Angular constructs using the *constructor* of the class. When a component is instantiated, Angular will automatically resolve and provide the required dependencies based on their registered providers.

To inject a dependency, we simply declare it as a parameter in the constructor of our component or service. For example, if we have a *UserService* that needs an instance of the *HttpClient* service, we can inject it like this:

```
import { HttpClient } from '@angular/common/http';

constructor(private httpClient: HttpClient) {
  // ...
}
```

Angular will automatically create an instance of *HttpClient* and provide it to our *UserService* when it is instantiated.

3.3.3 Registering Providers

To enable dependency injection, we need to register providers in Angular. Providers are responsible for creating and managing instances of our dependencies. We can register providers at different levels, such as at the component level, module level, or even globally.

At the component level, we can specify the providers directly in the *@Component* decorator. For example:

```
@Component({
  selector: 'app-user',
  templateUrl: './user.component.html',
  providers: [UserService]
})
export class UserComponent {
  // ...
}
```

In this example, we are registering the *UserService* as a provider for the *UserComponent*. This means that whenever an instance of *UserComponent* is created, Angular will also create an instance of *UserService* and inject it into the component.

At the module level, we can register providers in the *providers* array of the *@NgModule* decorator. This allows us to share the same instance of a service across multiple components within the module.

```
@NgModule({
  declarations: [AppComponent, UserComponent],
  providers: [UserService],
  imports: [BrowserModule],
  bootstrap: [AppComponent]
})
export class AppModule {
  // ...
}
```

In this example, the *UserService* is registered as a provider at the module level. This means that any component within the *AppModule* can inject and use the same instance of *UserService*.

3.3.4 Hierarchical Injection

Angular follows a hierarchical injection system, where dependencies can be resolved at different levels in the application's component tree. This allows us to provide different instances of a service at different levels, depending on our requirements.

When a component requests a dependency, Angular first checks if the component itself has a provider for that dependency. If not, it traverses up the component tree until it finds a provider or reaches the root module.

This hierarchical injection system allows us to override providers at different levels, providing flexibility and customization in our application.

3.3.5 Using Injection Tokens

In some cases, we may need to provide dependencies that are not classes or services. For example, we might want to provide a configuration object or a string value. In such cases, we can use injection tokens.

An injection token is a unique identifier that Angular uses to resolve dependencies. We can create an injection token using the *InjectionToken* class provided by Angular.

```
import { InjectionToken } from '@angular/core';

export const API_URL = new InjectionToken<string>('API_URL'
);
```

In this example, we create an injection token called *API_URL* of type *string*. We can then use this token to provide and inject the API URL value throughout our application.

```
import { Component, Inject } from '@angular/core';
import { API_URL } from './app.tokens';

@Component({
  selector: 'app-user',
  templateUrl: './user.component.html',
  providers: [{ provide: API_URL, useValue: 'https://api.ex
ample.com' }]
})
export class UserComponent {
  constructor(@Inject(API_URL) private apiUrl: string) {
    // ...
  }
}
```

In this example, we provide the value *'https://api.example.com'* for the *API_URL* token at the component level. The value can then be injected into the *UserComponent* using the *@Inject* decorator.

3.3.6 Summary

Dependency injection is a powerful feature of Angular that allows us to create modular, reusable, and testable code. By leveraging dependency injection, we can easily manage and provide the dependencies our components and services require. This promotes code flexibility, maintainability, and separation of concerns in our Angular applications.

3.4 Reusable Services

In Angular, services play a crucial role in providing a way to share data and functionality across different components. They act as a central hub for managing data, performing operations, and interacting with external resources. Reusable services are an essential part of building scalable and maintainable Angular applications.

3.4.1 Introduction to Services

Services in Angular are singleton objects that can be injected into components, modules, or other services. They are typically used to encapsulate business logic, handle data operations, or interact with external APIs. By separating the logic into services, you can achieve better code organization, reusability, and testability.

3.4.2 Creating a Service

To create a service in Angular, you can use the *@Injectable* decorator provided by the Angular framework. This decorator marks the class as a service and allows it to be injected into other components or services. Here's an example of creating a simple service:

```
import { Injectable } from '@angular/core';

@Injectable({
  providedIn: 'root'
})
export class DataService {
  private data: string[] = [];

  addData(value: string) {
    this.data.push(value);
  }

  getData(): string[] {
    return this.data;
  }
}
```

In the above example, we define a *DataService* class and mark it with the *@Injectable* decorator. The *providedIn: 'root'* option ensures that the service is available throughout the application. Inside the service, we have a private *data* array and two methods: *addData* to add data to the array and *getData* to retrieve the data.

3.4.3 Injecting a Service

Once a service is created, it can be injected into components or other services using Angular's dependency injection mechanism. To inject a service, you need to specify it as a constructor parameter in the component or service where it is required. Angular will automatically resolve and provide the instance of the service.

```
import { Component } from '@angular/core';
import { DataService } from './data.service';

@Component({
  selector: 'app-example',
  template: `
    <button (click)="addData()">Add Data</button>
    <ul>
      <li *ngFor="let item of data">{{ item }}</li>
    </ul>
  `
})
export class ExampleComponent {
  data: string[] = [];

  constructor(private dataService: DataService) {}

  addData() {
    this.dataService.addData('New Data');
    this.data = this.dataService.getData();
  }
}
```

In the above example, we have an *ExampleComponent* that depends on the *DataService*. We inject the *DataService* by specifying it as a constructor parameter with the *private* access modifier. Inside the *addData* method, we call the *addData* method of the service to add data and then retrieve the updated data using the *getData* method.

3.4.4 Providing a Service

Angular provides different ways to provide a service. The most common approach is to provide the service at the root level using the *providedIn: 'root'* option in the *@Injectable* decorator. This makes the service available throughout the application.

Alternatively, you can provide the service at the component level by specifying it in the *providers* array of the component's metadata. This creates a new instance of the service for each component and its child components.

```
import { Component } from '@angular/core';
import { DataService } from './data.service';

@Component({
  selector: 'app-example',
  template: `
    <button (click)="addData()">Add Data</button>
    <ul>
      <li *ngFor="let item of data">{{ item }}</li>
    </ul>
  `,
  providers: [DataService]
})
export class ExampleComponent {
  // ...
}
```

In the above example, we provide the *DataService* at the component level by including it in the *providers* array of the *ExampleComponent*. This creates a separate instance of the service for each instance of the component.

3.4.5 Sharing Data between Components using a Service

One of the main benefits of using services is the ability to share data between components. By storing the data in a service, multiple components can access and modify it. This allows for better communication and coordination between different parts of the application.

```
import { Component } from '@angular/core';
import { DataService } from './data.service';

@Component({
  selector: 'app-component-a',
  template: `
    <button (click)="addData()">Add Data</button>
  `
})
export class ComponentA {
  constructor(private dataService: DataService) {}

  addData() {
    this.dataService.addData('New Data');
  }
}

@Component({
  selector: 'app-component-b',
  template: `
    <ul>
      <li *ngFor="let item of data">{{ item }}</li>
    </ul>
  `
})
export class ComponentB {
  data: string[] = [];

  constructor(private dataService: DataService) {
    this.data = this.dataService.getData();
  }
}
```

In the above example, we have two components: *ComponentA* and *ComponentB*. *ComponentA* adds data to the *DataService* using the *addData* method, while *ComponentB* retrieves the data using the *getData* method. Both components share the same instance of the *DataService*, allowing them to communicate and share data.

3.4.6 Conclusion

Reusable services are a powerful feature of Angular that enable the sharing of data and functionality across different components. By encapsulating logic in services, you can achieve better code organization, reusability, and testability. Services play a crucial role in building scalable and maintainable Angular applications.

4 Routing and Navigation

4.1 Introduction to Angular Routing

Routing is an essential part of building modern web applications. It allows us to navigate between different views or pages within a single-page application (SPA) without the need for a full page reload. Angular provides a powerful routing module that makes it easy to implement navigation and handle different routes within our application.

In this section, we will explore the basics of Angular routing and learn how to set up routes for our application. We will also cover how to navigate between routes and introduce the concept of route guards for controlling access to certain routes.

4.1.1 What is Angular Routing?

Angular routing is a mechanism that allows us to define and manage different routes within our application. It enables us to map URLs to specific components, providing a seamless navigation experience for users. With Angular routing, we can create SPAs that have multiple views or pages, each represented by a different component.

4.1.2 Setting up Routes

To get started with Angular routing, we need to set up the necessary configuration. First, we need to import the *RouterModule* from *@angular/router* and add it to our application's module imports. This will enable the routing functionality for our application.

Next, we define our routes using the *Routes* array. Each route consists of a path and a component. The path represents the URL segment that will trigger the display of the associated component. For example, if we have a route with the path *'home'* and a component *HomeComponent*, navigating to *'/home'* will display the *HomeComponent*.

We can also define additional properties for each route, such as route parameters or data that needs to be passed to the component. These properties can be accessed within the component using the *ActivatedRoute* service.

4.1.3 Navigating between Routes

Once we have set up our routes, we can navigate between them programmatically or through user interactions. Angular provides the *Router* service, which we can inject into our components to handle navigation.

To navigate to a specific route, we can use the *navigate* method of the *Router* service. We pass the desired route path as a parameter to this method. For example, *this.router.navigate(['/home'])* will navigate to the *'/home'* route.

We can also navigate to a route with route parameters by passing an object as the second parameter to the *navigate* method. This object should contain the necessary route parameters. For example, *this.router.navigate(['/user', userId])* will navigate to the *'/user/:userId'* route, where *:userId* is a route parameter.

4.1.4 Route Guards

Route guards are used to control access to certain routes in our application. They allow us to implement authentication and authorization logic to protect sensitive routes from unauthorized access.

Angular provides several types of route guards, including *CanActivate*, *CanActivateChild*, *CanDeactivate*, and *Resolve*. These guards can be implemented as services and attached to specific routes or used globally for all routes.

The *CanActivate* guard is used to determine if a user is allowed to access a particular route. It can be used to check if the user is authenticated or has the necessary permissions. If the guard returns *true*, the navigation continues; otherwise, the user is redirected to a different route.

The *CanActivateChild* guard is similar to *CanActivate*, but it is used to protect child routes. It allows us to define guards that apply to all child routes of a specific parent route.

The *CanDeactivate* guard is used to determine if a user is allowed to leave a particular route. It can be used to prompt the user for confirmation before leaving a form or unsaved changes.

The *Resolve* guard is used to fetch data before activating a route. It allows us to load data from a server or perform any necessary operations before displaying the route's component.

By using route guards, we can ensure that our application's routes are protected and that users have the appropriate permissions to access certain views.

In the next section, we will dive deeper into setting up routes and explore more advanced routing concepts, such as child routes and lazy loading.

4.1.5 Summary

In this section, we learned about the basics of Angular routing. We explored how to set up routes for our application and navigate between them using the *Router* service. We also introduced the concept of route guards for controlling access to certain routes. With this knowledge, we can now start building more complex navigation structures within our Angular applications.

4.2 Setting up Routes

Routing is an essential part of building modern web applications. It allows us to navigate between different views or pages within our application without having to reload the entire page. In Angular, routing is handled by the Angular Router module, which provides a powerful and flexible way to define and manage routes.

4.2.1 Configuring the Router Module

To get started with routing in Angular, we need to configure the Router module. This module is responsible for mapping URLs to components and handling navigation between different routes.

The first step is to import the necessary modules from the *@angular/router* package. In your Angular project, open the *app.module.ts* file and add the following imports:

```
import { RouterModule, Routes } from '@angular/router';
```

Next, we need to define the routes for our application. A route is an object that maps a URL path to a component. In the same *app.module.ts* file, add the following code:

```
const routes: Routes = [
  { path: '', component: HomeComponent },
  { path: 'about', component: AboutComponent },
  { path: 'contact', component: ContactComponent },
];
```

In this example, we have defined three routes: the root route (''), the /about route, and the /contact route. Each route is associated with a specific component.

Now, we need to configure the Router module to use these routes. Add the following code to the *imports* array in the *@NgModule* decorator:

```
RouterModule.forRoot(routes)
```

This method takes the routes array we defined earlier and configures the Router module to use these routes.

4.2.2 Displaying the Router Outlet

To display the components associated with different routes, we need to add a *<router-outlet>* element to our application's template. Open the *app.component.html* file and add the following code:

```
<router-outlet></router-outlet>
```

The *<router-outlet>* element acts as a placeholder where the Router module will render the component associated with the current route.

4.2.3 Navigating between Routes

Now that we have set up our routes and added the *<router-outlet>* element, we can navigate between different routes in our application.

To navigate to a specific route, we can use the *routerLink* directive provided by the Router module. This directive allows us to create links that trigger navigation to a specific route.

In your application's template, you can add the following code to create a navigation menu:

```
<nav>
  <a routerLink="/">Home</a>
  <a routerLink="/about">About</a>
  <a routerLink="/contact">Contact</a>
</nav>
```

In this example, we have created three links: one for the home route, one for the about route, and one for the contact route. When a user clicks on one of these links, the Router module will navigate to the corresponding route and render the associated component.

4.2.4 Route Parameters

In addition to static routes, Angular's Router module also supports dynamic routes with parameters. Route parameters allow us to pass data to a component based on the current route.

To define a route with parameters, we can use the *:paramName* syntax. For example, let's say we want to create a route for displaying a user's profile. We can define the following route:

```
{ path: 'profile/:id', component: ProfileComponent }
```

In this example, the *:id* parameter represents the user's ID. When navigating to a URL like */profile/123*, the Router module will extract the value *123* from the URL and pass it as a parameter to the *ProfileComponent*.

To access the parameter in the component, we can use the *ActivatedRoute* service provided by the Router module. This service gives us access to the current route's parameters.

```
import { ActivatedRoute } from '@angular/router';

constructor(private route: ActivatedRoute) {}

ngOnInit() {
  this.route.params.subscribe(params => {
    const id = params['id'];
    // Use the id parameter in your component logic
  });
}
```

In this example, we subscribe to the *params* observable provided by the *ActivatedRoute* service. Whenever the route parameters change, the callback function will be called, allowing us to access the updated parameter values.

4.2.5 Route Guards

Route guards are a powerful feature provided by the Angular Router module. They allow us to control access to routes based on certain conditions. For example, we can use route guards to prevent unauthorized users from accessing certain routes or to ensure that a user is authenticated before accessing protected routes.

There are several types of route guards available in Angular:

- **CanActivate**: Allows or denies access to a route based on a condition.

- **CanActivateChild**: Similar to *CanActivate,* but applies to child routes.

- **CanDeactivate**: Allows or denies navigation away from a route based on a condition.

- **Resolve**: Fetches data before activating a route.

- **CanLoad**: Allows or denies loading of a lazy-loaded module based on a condition.

To use a route guard, we need to implement the corresponding interface and provide the guard in the route configuration.

For example, let's say we want to create a route guard to prevent unauthorized users from accessing a protected route. We can define the following guard:

```
import { Injectable } from '@angular/core';
import { CanActivate, ActivatedRouteSnapshot, RouterStateSn
apshot, UrlTree, Router } from '@angular/router';
import { AuthService } from './auth.service';

@Injectable({
  providedIn: 'root'
})
export class AuthGuard implements CanActivate {
  constructor(private authService: AuthService, private rou
ter: Router) {}

  canActivate(
    next: ActivatedRouteSnapshot,
    state: RouterStateSnapshot): boolean | UrlTree {
    if (this.authService.isAuthenticated()) {
      return true;
    } else {
      return this.router.parseUrl('/login');
    }
  }
}
```

In this example, the AuthGuard implements the CanActivate interface. The canActivate method is called by the Router module to determine whether the user is allowed to access the route.

To use the **AuthGuard**, we need to provide it in the route configuration:

```
{ path: 'profile', component: ProfileComponent, canActivate
: [AuthGuard] }
```

In this example, the AuthGuard is applied to the /profile route. If the user is not authenticated, the Router module will redirect them to the /login route.

Route guards provide a powerful way to control access to routes and enforce security policies in our application.

4.2.6 Conclusion

In this section, we learned how to set up routes in an Angular application. We configured the Router module, displayed components using the `<router-outlet>` element, and learned how to navigate between routes using the *routerLink* directive. We also explored route parameters and how to access them in our components. Finally, we discussed route guards and how they can be used to control access to routes based on certain conditions. With this knowledge, you can now start building more complex and dynamic web applications using Angular's powerful routing capabilities.

4.3 Navigating between Routes

In this section, we will explore how to navigate between routes in an Angular application. Routing is an essential feature of modern web applications, allowing users to move between different views or pages without having to reload the entire application. Angular provides a powerful routing module that makes it easy to implement navigation in your application.

4.3.1 Configuring Routes

Before we can navigate between routes, we need to set up the routes in our application. In Angular, routes are defined using the *RouterModule* and *Routes* classes. The *RouterModule* is imported from *@angular/router* and is responsible for providing the routing functionality to our application. The *Routes* class is an array of route definitions, where each route definition specifies a path and the component to be displayed when that path is accessed.

To configure routes in our application, we need to import the *RouterModule* and call the *forRoot* method, passing in the array of route definitions. This should be done in the root module of our application, typically in the *AppModule*.

Here's an example of how to configure routes in an Angular application:

```
import { NgModule } from '@angular/core';
import { RouterModule, Routes } from '@angular/router';

import { HomeComponent } from './home.component';
import { AboutComponent } from './about.component';

const routes: Routes = [
  { path: '', component: HomeComponent },
  { path: 'about', component: AboutComponent },
];

@NgModule({
  imports: [RouterModule.forRoot(routes)],
  exports: [RouterModule]
})
export class AppRoutingModule { }
```

In this example, we have defined two routes: the root route, which maps to the *HomeComponent*, and the */about* route, which maps to the *AboutComponent*. The *path* property specifies the URL path for each route, and the *component* property specifies the component to be displayed when that path is accessed.

4.3.2 Navigating with the RouterLink Directive

Once we have configured our routes, we can use the *RouterLink* directive to create links that navigate to different routes in our application. The *RouterLink* directive is provided by the *RouterModule* and allows us to bind a link to a specific route.

To use the *RouterLink* directive, we simply add it to an anchor tag (*<a>*) and bind it to the desired route using the *routerLink* attribute. When the link is clicked, Angular will automatically navigate to the specified route.

Here's an example of how to use the *RouterLink* directive:

```
<nav>
  <a routerLink="/">Home</a>
  <a routerLink="/about">About</a>
</nav>
```

In this example, we have created two links: one for the home route and one for the about route. When the user clicks on either of these links, Angular will navigate to the corresponding route and display the associated component.

4.3.3 Navigating Programmatically

In addition to using the *RouterLink* directive, we can also navigate programmatically using the *Router* service provided by the *@angular/router* package. The *Router* service allows us to navigate to a specific route using its *navigate* method.

To navigate programmatically, we first need to inject the *Router* service into our component. We can then call the *navigate* method and pass in the desired route as a string or an array of route segments.

Here's an example of how to navigate programmatically:

```
import { Component } from '@angular/core';
import { Router } from '@angular/router';

@Component({
  selector: 'app-home',
  template: `
    <button (click)="goToAbout()">Go to About</button>
`
})
export class HomeComponent {
  constructor(private router: Router) {}

  goToAbout() {
    this.router.navigate(['/about']);
  }
}
```

In this example, we have a button that, when clicked, triggers the *goToAbout* method. Inside this method, we use the *Router* service to navigate to the */about* route.

4.3.4 Passing Parameters to Routes

Sometimes, we may need to pass parameters to a route, such as an ID or a query string. Angular provides a way to pass parameters to routes using route parameters and query parameters.

Route parameters are placeholders in the route path that are replaced with actual values when the route is accessed. To define a route parameter, we use the colon (:) followed by the parameter name in the route path. We can then access the parameter value in the component using the *ActivatedRoute* service provided by the *@angular/router* package.

Query parameters, on the other hand, are key-value pairs that are appended to the route URL. They are typically used for optional parameters or for passing additional data to the route. We can access query parameters in the component using the *ActivatedRoute* service as well.

Here's an example of how to define and access route parameters and query parameters:

```
import { Component } from '@angular/core';
import { ActivatedRoute } from '@angular/router';

@Component({
  selector: 'app-product',
  template: `
    <h2>Product Details</h2>
    <p>Product ID: {{ productId }}</p>
    <p>Category: {{ category }}</p>
  `
})
export class ProductComponent {
  productId: string;
  category: string;

  constructor(private route: ActivatedRoute) {}

  ngOnInit() {
    this.route.params.subscribe(params => {
      this.productId = params['id'];
    });

    this.route.queryParams.subscribe(params => {
      this.category = params['category'];
    });
  }
}
```

In this example, we have a *ProductComponent* that displays the details of a product. The component uses the *ActivatedRoute* service to access the route parameters and query parameters. Inside the *ngOnInit* method, we subscribe to the *params* and *queryParams* observables to get the parameter values and assign them to the component properties.

With the knowledge of navigating between routes and passing parameters, you can now create more dynamic and interactive web applications using Angular's powerful routing module.

4.4 Route Guards

In Chapter 4, we explored the basics of Angular routing and learned how to set up routes and navigate between them. However, there may be scenarios where we want to control access to certain routes based on certain conditions. This is where route guards come into play.

Route guards are used to protect routes and control access to them. They allow us to implement logic that determines whether a user is allowed to navigate to a particular route or not. There are several types of route guards available in Angular, including:

4.4.1 CanActivate

The *CanActivate* guard is used to determine if a user is allowed to activate a particular route. It is typically used to implement authentication and authorization logic. For example, we can use this guard to check if a user is logged in before allowing them to access certain routes. If the user is not authenticated, we can redirect them to a login page or display an error message.

To implement the *CanActivate* guard, we need to create a service that implements the *CanActivate* interface. This service should have a *canActivate* method that returns a boolean or a promise/observable that resolves to a boolean. If the method returns *true*, the route is activated. If it returns *false*, the route is blocked.

4.4.2 CanActivateChild

Similar to *CanActivate*, the *CanActivateChild* guard is used to determine if a user is allowed to activate child routes of a particular route. It is useful when we have nested routes and want to control access to the child routes based on certain conditions. The implementation of *CanActivateChild* is similar to *CanActivate*, where we create a service that implements the *CanActivateChild* interface.

4.4.3 CanDeactivate

The *CanDeactivate* guard is used to determine if a user is allowed to deactivate a particular route. It is typically used to implement confirmation dialogs or prevent users from accidentally navigating away from a form with unsaved changes. To implement the *CanDeactivate* guard, we need to create a service that implements the *CanDeactivate* interface. This service should have a *canDeactivate* method that returns a boolean or a promise/observable that resolves to a boolean.

4.4.4 Resolve

The *Resolve* guard is used to fetch data before activating a route. It is useful when we need to load data from a server or perform some asynchronous operation before displaying the route's content. The *Resolve* guard allows us to fetch the necessary data and pass it to the route's component as a resolved value. This ensures that the data is available when the component is initialized.

To implement the *Resolve* guard, we need to create a service that implements the *Resolve* interface. This service should have a *resolve* method that returns the resolved data or a promise/observable that resolves to the data.

4.4.5 CanLoad

The *CanLoad* guard is used to determine if a user is allowed to load a lazy-loaded module. It is typically used to implement lazy loading with authentication and authorization. If a user is not allowed to load a particular module, we can prevent the module from being loaded and display an error message or redirect the user to a different page.

To implement the *CanLoad* guard, we need to create a service that implements the *CanLoad* interface. This service should have a *canLoad* method that returns a boolean or a promise/observable that resolves to a boolean.

Route guards provide a powerful mechanism for controlling access to routes and implementing various security features in our Angular applications. By using the appropriate guard for each scenario, we can ensure that our routes are protected and that users can only access the routes they are authorized to access.

In the next section, we will explore some advanced topics in Angular, including reactive programming with RxJS, state management with NgRx, and performance optimization.

5 Advanced Topics

5.1 Reactive Programming with RxJS

Reactive Programming is a programming paradigm that allows developers to build applications that react to changes in data and events. It provides a way to handle asynchronous operations and manage complex data flows in a more efficient and declarative manner. In the context of Angular, Reactive Programming is often used with RxJS, a powerful library that provides a set of tools for working with reactive streams.

5.1.1 Introduction to Reactive Programming

Reactive Programming is based on the concept of streams, which are sequences of events or values over time. These streams can be observed, transformed, and combined to create more complex streams. RxJS provides a set of operators that allow developers to manipulate these streams and perform various operations such as filtering, mapping, and reducing.

One of the key benefits of Reactive Programming is its ability to handle asynchronous operations in a more elegant way. Instead of using callbacks or promises, developers can use Observables, which are a core concept in RxJS. Observables represent streams of data that can be observed by subscribers. They can emit values over time, and subscribers can react to these values by defining functions that are executed whenever a new value is emitted.

5.1.2 Working with Observables

In Angular, Observables are used extensively for handling asynchronous operations such as HTTP requests, user input, and event handling. The Angular framework itself makes use of Observables in many of its core features, such as the HttpClient module and the event system.

To work with Observables in Angular, you need to import the necessary functions and operators from the RxJS library. You can then create Observables using functions such as *of*, *from*, or by transforming other data sources into Observables using operators like *map* or *filter*.

Once you have an Observable, you can subscribe to it to start receiving values. The *subscribe* method takes one or more functions as arguments, which will be called whenever a new value is emitted by the Observable. These functions can be used to process the emitted values, update the application state, or trigger other actions.

5.1.3 Operators and Transformation

RxJS provides a wide range of operators that allow you to transform, filter, and combine Observables. These operators can be used to perform operations such as mapping values, filtering out unwanted values, merging multiple streams, or combining the latest values from multiple streams.

Some commonly used operators include *map*, *filter*, *mergeMap*, *switchMap*, and *combineLatest*. The *map* operator allows you to transform the values emitted by an Observable, while the *filter* operator allows you to filter out unwanted values based on a condition. The *mergeMap* and *switchMap* operators are used to handle scenarios where you need to perform asynchronous operations and combine the results. The *combineLatest* operator allows you to combine the latest values from multiple streams into a single stream.

5.1.4 Handling Errors and Cancellation

In addition to handling data streams, RxJS also provides mechanisms for handling errors and cancellation. Observables can emit error values, which can be caught and handled using the *catchError* operator. This allows you to gracefully handle errors and provide fallback behavior when something goes wrong.

Observables also support cancellation through the use of the *unsubscribe* method. When you subscribe to an Observable, you receive a subscription object that can be used to cancel the subscription and stop receiving values. This is particularly useful when dealing with long-running operations or when you no longer need to observe a stream.

5.1.5 Using RxJS in Angular Applications

Angular provides built-in support for working with RxJS through its integration with the Angular HttpClient module and the event system. When making HTTP requests using the HttpClient module, you can use the *pipe* method to apply RxJS operators to the response stream. This allows you to transform the response data, handle errors, and perform other operations before consuming the data in your application.

In addition to the HttpClient module, you can also use RxJS to handle user input and events in your Angular components. By subscribing to Observables representing user input or events, you can react to changes in real-time and update the application state accordingly.

5.1.6 Benefits and Best Practices

Reactive Programming with RxJS offers several benefits for Angular developers. It provides a more declarative and concise way to handle asynchronous operations, making the code easier to read and maintain. It also allows for better separation of concerns, as complex data flows can be encapsulated in reusable streams.

When working with RxJS in Angular, it is important to follow some best practices. It is recommended to keep the number of subscriptions to a minimum and use operators like *switchMap* or *mergeMap* to handle complex data flows. It is also important to properly handle errors and cancellation to ensure the application behaves correctly in all scenarios.

By mastering Reactive Programming with RxJS, you can unlock the full potential of Angular and build more efficient and responsive web applications.

5.2 State Management with NgRx

State management is a crucial aspect of building complex web applications. As applications grow in size and complexity, managing the state becomes more challenging. In Angular, one popular solution for state management is NgRx.

NgRx is a library that implements the Redux pattern for Angular applications. Redux is a predictable state container that helps manage the state of an application in a consistent and scalable way. It provides a single source of truth for the application state and enforces a strict unidirectional data flow.

5.2.1 Introduction to NgRx

NgRx is built on top of RxJS, which is a powerful library for reactive programming in JavaScript. It leverages the concepts of actions, reducers, and selectors to manage the state of an application.

Actions represent events that occur in the application. They are dispatched to trigger state changes. Actions are plain JavaScript objects with a type property that describes the action being performed.

Reducers are pure functions that take the current state and an action as input and return a new state. They are responsible for handling actions and updating the state accordingly. Reducers should always return a new state object instead of modifying the existing state.

Selectors are functions that derive specific pieces of state from the global state. They provide a convenient way to access and transform the state in a predictable manner. Selectors can be used to compute derived state or to filter and transform data.

5.2.2 Setting up NgRx

To use NgRx in an Angular application, you need to install the required packages and set up the necessary files and folders. The core packages required for NgRx are *@ngrx/store* and *@ngrx/effects*.

Once the packages are installed, you need to create the necessary files and folders for actions, reducers, and effects. Actions are typically defined in a separate file, while reducers and effects are organized in their respective folders.

To integrate NgRx with Angular, you also need to configure the store module in the application's root module. The store module provides a central place to manage the application state and allows components to access and update the state.

5.2.3 Creating Actions and Reducers

Actions are the building blocks of NgRx. They represent the different events or user interactions that can occur in the application. Actions are defined as classes or functions that return an action object with a type property.

Reducers are responsible for handling actions and updating the state. They are pure functions that take the current state and an action as input and return a new state. Reducers should be defined as separate functions and combined using the *combineReducers* function provided by NgRx.

5.2.4 Dispatching Actions and Updating the State

To trigger state changes, actions need to be dispatched. Dispatching an action is as simple as calling a function or method that dispatches the action object. Actions can be dispatched from components, services, or effects.

When an action is dispatched, it goes through the reducers, which handle the action and update the state accordingly. The reducers should always return a new state object instead of modifying the existing state. NgRx takes care of immutability and ensures that the state is updated in a predictable manner.

5.2.5 Selecting State with Selectors

Selectors provide a convenient way to access and transform the state in a predictable manner. They allow you to derive specific pieces of state from the global state. Selectors can be used to compute derived state or to filter and transform data.

Selectors are defined as functions that take the global state as input and return a specific piece of state. They can be composed together to create more complex selectors. Selectors are memoized, meaning that they cache the result and only recalculate it if the input state changes.

5.2.6 Handling Side Effects with Effects

Effects are used to handle side effects, such as making HTTP requests or interacting with external services. They are defined as classes that listen for specific actions and perform asynchronous operations in response to those actions.

Effects are responsible for dispatching new actions based on the outcome of the asynchronous operations. They can be used to trigger additional actions, update the state, or perform other side effects. Effects are registered in the application's root module using the *EffectsModule.forRoot()* function.

5.2.7 Testing NgRx

Testing NgRx applications involves testing the actions, reducers, selectors, and effects. Actions can be tested by creating instances of the action classes and asserting that the resulting action objects have the expected properties.

Reducers can be tested by calling the reducer functions with different input states and actions and asserting that the resulting states are as expected. Selectors can be tested by calling the selector functions with different input states and asserting that the returned values are correct.

Effects can be tested by creating instances of the effect classes and providing mock dependencies. The effects can then be triggered by dispatching actions and asserting that the resulting actions or state changes are as expected.

5.2.8 Best Practices for NgRx

When using NgRx, it is important to follow some best practices to ensure a clean and maintainable codebase. Here are some recommendations:

- Keep the state structure flat and normalized to improve performance and simplify state updates.
- Use selectors to derive specific pieces of state instead of accessing the state directly.
- Use the *createAction* function provided by NgRx to define actions, as it helps enforce type safety and reduces boilerplate code.
- Use the *createReducer* function provided by NgRx to define reducers, as it simplifies the reducer logic and reduces the chances of introducing bugs.
- Use effects sparingly and only for handling side effects. Keep the business logic in reducers and selectors.

- Use the *createFeatureSelector* function provided by NgRx to define feature selectors, as it helps organize the state and makes it easier to work with.

By following these best practices, you can ensure that your NgRx code is clean, maintainable, and scalable.

In this section, we covered the basics of NgRx, including actions, reducers, selectors, and effects. We also discussed how to set up NgRx in an Angular application and provided some best practices for using NgRx effectively. NgRx is a powerful tool for managing the state of Angular applications and can greatly simplify the development process.

5.3 Performance Optimization

Performance optimization is a crucial aspect of building web applications, especially when it comes to large-scale projects. In this section, we will explore various techniques and best practices to optimize the performance of Angular applications. By implementing these strategies, you can ensure that your application runs smoothly, loads quickly, and provides a seamless user experience.

5.3.1 Lazy Loading

Lazy loading is a technique that allows you to load modules and components on-demand, rather than loading everything upfront. This can significantly improve the initial load time of your application, as only the necessary resources are loaded when they are needed. Angular provides built-in support for lazy loading through its routing module.

To implement lazy loading, you need to define separate routes for each module or component that you want to load lazily. When a user navigates to a route associated with a lazy-loaded module, Angular will dynamically load the module and its dependencies. This approach helps reduce the initial bundle size and improves the overall performance of your application.

5.3.2 Change Detection Strategies

Angular's change detection mechanism is responsible for detecting and updating the UI when the application's state changes. By default, Angular uses a strategy called "OnPush" for change detection. However, you can optimize the performance of your application by explicitly specifying the change detection strategy for individual components.

The "OnPush" change detection strategy tells Angular to only check for changes in a component's input properties and not to perform a deep check of the component's entire template. This can significantly reduce the number of unnecessary checks and improve the performance of your application.

To specify the change detection strategy for a component, you need to set the *changeDetection* property in the component's metadata to *ChangeDetectionStrategy.OnPush*. This tells Angular to use the "OnPush" strategy for that component.

5.3.3 Angular Universal

Angular Universal is a server-side rendering (SSR) solution provided by Angular. It allows you to render your application on the server and send the pre-rendered HTML to the client, improving the initial load time and search engine optimization (SEO) of your application.

By using Angular Universal, you can serve fully rendered HTML to the client, which eliminates the need for the client to wait for the JavaScript bundle to load and execute before rendering the page. This can significantly improve the perceived performance of your application, especially on slower network connections.

To implement Angular Universal, you need to set up a server-side rendering environment and configure your application to support server-side rendering. Angular provides a set of APIs and tools to simplify this process and make it easier to implement server-side rendering in your Angular application.

5.3.4 Tree Shaking

Tree shaking is a technique used by modern JavaScript bundlers, such as Webpack, to eliminate dead code from the final bundle. It analyzes the application's dependency graph and removes any unused code, reducing the bundle size and improving the performance of your application.

To take advantage of tree shaking in your Angular application, you need to ensure that your code is written in a way that allows the bundler to perform effective dead code elimination. This includes using ES6 modules, avoiding side effects in your code, and using Angular's dependency injection system correctly.

By optimizing your code for tree shaking, you can significantly reduce the size of your application's JavaScript bundle, resulting in faster load times and improved performance.

5.3.5 Performance Monitoring and Profiling

Monitoring and profiling the performance of your Angular application is essential to identify bottlenecks and areas for improvement. Angular provides built-in tools and APIs that allow you to measure and analyze the performance of your application.

The Angular Performance Explorer is a tool that provides real-time performance metrics, such as CPU and memory usage, network requests, and rendering performance. It allows you to monitor the performance of your application during development and identify any performance issues.

In addition to the built-in tools, there are also third-party tools and libraries available that can help you profile and optimize the performance of your Angular application. These tools provide more detailed insights into the performance characteristics of your application and can help you identify specific areas that need improvement.

By regularly monitoring and profiling the performance of your Angular application, you can ensure that it remains fast and responsive, even as it grows in complexity.

5.3.6 Conclusion

In this section, we explored various techniques and best practices to optimize the performance of Angular applications. By implementing lazy loading, using the "OnPush" change detection strategy, leveraging Angular Universal for server-side rendering, optimizing for tree shaking, and monitoring and profiling the performance of your application, you can ensure that your Angular application delivers a fast and seamless user experience. Remember to regularly review and optimize the performance of your application as it evolves to maintain its optimal performance.

6 Testing and Debugging

6.1 Unit Testing with Jasmine

Unit testing is an essential part of the software development process. It allows developers to verify that individual units of code, such as functions or classes, are working correctly. In the context of Angular applications, unit testing ensures that components, services, and other Angular constructs behave as expected.

6.1.1 Introduction to Unit Testing

Unit testing is a software testing technique that focuses on testing individual units of code in isolation. The goal is to verify that each unit performs as intended and produces the expected output given a specific set of inputs. By testing units in isolation, developers can identify and fix issues early in the development process, leading to more reliable and maintainable code.

In the context of Angular applications, unit testing involves testing Angular components, services, and other Angular constructs. Angular provides a testing framework called Jasmine, which is widely used for unit testing Angular applications.

6.1.2 Getting Started with Jasmine

Jasmine is a behavior-driven development (BDD) testing framework for JavaScript. It provides a clean and expressive syntax for writing tests and comes with a rich set of matchers and utilities for assertions.

To get started with Jasmine, you need to set up a testing environment for your Angular application. Angular provides a testing module called `@angular/core/testing` that simplifies the process of setting up and running tests.

First, you need to install Jasmine and its dependencies. You can do this by running the following command in your project directory:

```
npm install jasmine @types/jasmine karma-jasmine karma-chro
me-launcher --save-dev
```

Next, you need to configure Karma, a test runner for JavaScript, to run your Jasmine tests. Karma allows you to execute your tests in real browsers or headless environments.

To configure Karma, you need to create a *karma.conf.js* file in your project directory. This file specifies the files to include in the test bundle, the browsers to use for testing, and other configuration options.

Here's an example *karma.conf.js* file:

```
module.exports = function (config) {
  config.set({
    frameworks: ['jasmine'],
    files: [
      'src/**/*.spec.ts'
    ],
    browsers: ['Chrome'],
    reporters: ['progress'],
    singleRun: true
  });
};
```

In this example, we configure Karma to use Jasmine as the testing framework, include all *.spec.ts* files in the *src* directory for testing, use Chrome as the browser for testing, and report the test results in the console.

6.1.3 Writing Unit Tests with Jasmine

Once you have set up the testing environment, you can start writing unit tests using Jasmine. Jasmine provides a set of functions and matchers that allow you to define test suites and test cases.

A test suite is a group of related test cases that test a specific unit of code. It is defined using the *describe* function, which takes a description of the suite and a callback function that contains the test cases.

Here's an example of a test suite for a simple Angular component:

```
import { ComponentFixture, TestBed } from '@angular/core/te
sting';
import { MyComponent } from './my.component';

describe('MyComponent', () => {
  let component: MyComponent;
  let fixture: ComponentFixture<MyComponent>;

  beforeEach(async () => {
    await TestBed.configureTestingModule({
      declarations: [MyComponent]
    }).compileComponents();
  });

  beforeEach(() => {
    fixture = TestBed.createComponent(MyComponent);
    component = fixture.componentInstance;
    fixture.detectChanges();
  });

  it('should create', () => {
    expect(component).toBeTruthy();
  });

  it('should display the correct title', () => {
    const titleElement = fixture.nativeElement.querySelecto
r('h1');
    expect(titleElement.textContent).toContain('Hello, Angu
lar!');
  });
});
```

In this example, we define a test suite for a component called MyComponent. We use the *beforeEach* function to set up the testing environment before each test case. The *beforeEach* function is called once before each test case in the suite.

Each test case is defined using the *it* function, which takes a description of the test case and a callback function that contains the test logic. Inside the callback function, we use Jasmine's matchers to make assertions about the expected behavior of the component.

6.1.4 Running Unit Tests

To run the unit tests, you need to execute the following command in your project directory:

```
ng test
```

This command starts the Karma test runner and runs all the unit tests in your project. The test results are displayed in the console, indicating whether each test case passed or failed.

By default, Karma watches for changes in your source code and re-runs the tests whenever a change is detected. This allows you to continuously test your code as you make changes, ensuring that your tests are always up to date.

6.1.5 Testing Angular Services

In addition to testing Angular components, you can also test Angular services using Jasmine. Angular services are typically used to encapsulate business logic and provide data to components.

To test an Angular service, you can create a test suite similar to the one shown earlier for components. Inside the test cases, you can instantiate the service using the *TestBed.get* function and make assertions about its behavior.

Here's an example of a test suite for an Angular service:

```
import { TestBed } from '@angular/core/testing';
import { MyService } from './my.service';

describe('MyService', () => {
  let service: MyService;

  beforeEach(() => {
    TestBed.configureTestingModule({});
    service = TestBed.inject(MyService);
  });

  it('should be created', () => {
    expect(service).toBeTruthy();
  });

  it('should return the correct data', () => {
    const data = service.getData();
    expect(data).toEqual(['item1', 'item2', 'item3']);
  });
});
```

In this example, we define a test suite for a service called *MyService*. We use the *beforeEach* function to set up the testing environment before each test case. Inside the test cases, we use the *TestBed.inject* function to instantiate the service and make assertions about its behavior.

6.1.6 Conclusion

Unit testing is a crucial aspect of building reliable and maintainable Angular applications. Jasmine provides a powerful and expressive testing framework for writing unit tests in Angular. By following the principles and techniques outlined in this section, you can ensure that your Angular applications are thoroughly tested and free of bugs.

6.2 Setting up Karma

In this section, we will explore how to set up Karma, a popular test runner for JavaScript, to run unit tests for your Angular applications. Karma is a powerful tool that allows you to execute your tests in real browsers, making it easier to catch any browser-specific issues that may arise.

6.2.1 Installing Karma

To get started with Karma, you will need to install it globally on your machine. Open your terminal or command prompt and run the following command:

```
npm install -g karma
```

This will install Karma globally, allowing you to use it from any project.

6.2.2 Configuring Karma

Once Karma is installed, you need to set up a configuration file to define how your tests should be executed. In the root directory of your Angular project, create a file named *karma.conf.js*. This file will contain all the necessary configuration options for Karma.

Here is a basic example of a *karma.conf.js* file:

```
module.exports = function(config) {
  config.set({
    frameworks: ['jasmine'],
    files: [
      'src/**/*.spec.ts'
    ],
    preprocessors: {
      'src/**/*.spec.ts': ['webpack']
    },
    webpack: {
      // webpack configuration options
    },
    browsers: ['Chrome'],
    reporters: ['progress'],
    singleRun: true
  });
};
```

Let's go through each configuration option:

- *frameworks*: This option specifies the testing framework you want to use. In this example, we are using Jasmine, but you can also use other frameworks like Mocha or QUnit.

- *files*: This option specifies the files that should be included in the test runner. In this example, we are including all files with a *.spec.ts* extension in the *src* directory.

- *preprocessors*: This option allows you to preprocess your files before running the tests. In this example, we are using webpack as the preprocessor.

- *webpack*: This option allows you to specify the webpack configuration for your tests. You can include any necessary loaders or plugins here.

- *browsers*: This option specifies the browsers in which the tests should be executed. In this example, we are using Chrome, but you can also use other browsers like Firefox or Safari.

- *reporters*: This option specifies the reporters that should be used to display the test results. In this example, we are using the progress reporter, which displays a progress bar in the terminal.

- *singleRun*: This option specifies whether the tests should run once and then exit, or if they should keep running and watch for changes. In this example, we are running the tests once and then exiting.

6.2.3 Running Tests with Karma

To run your tests with Karma, open your terminal or command prompt and navigate to the root directory of your Angular project. Then, run the following command:

```
karma start
```

This will start the Karma test runner and execute your tests in the specified browsers. You will see the test results in the terminal or command prompt.

6.2.4 Writing Unit Tests

Now that Karma is set up, you can start writing unit tests for your Angular components, services, and other modules. Unit tests are an essential part of the development process as they help ensure the correctness of your code and catch any regressions.

To write unit tests in Angular, you can use the Jasmine testing framework, which provides a clean and expressive syntax for writing tests. Jasmine provides a set of functions and matchers that make it easy to define test suites and expectations.

Here is an example of a simple unit test for an Angular component:

```
import { ComponentFixture, TestBed } from '@angular/core/te
sting';
import { MyComponent } from './my.component';

describe('MyComponent', () => {
  let component: MyComponent;
  let fixture: ComponentFixture<MyComponent>;

  beforeEach(async () => {
    await TestBed.configureTestingModule({
      declarations: [ MyComponent ]
    })
    .compileComponents();
  });

  beforeEach(() => {
    fixture = TestBed.createComponent(MyComponent);
    component = fixture.componentInstance;
    fixture.detectChanges();
  });

  it('should create', () => {
    expect(component).toBeTruthy();
  });
});
```

In this example, we are importing the necessary testing utilities from *@angular/core/testing* and the component we want to test. We then define a test suite using the *describe* function and set up the necessary dependencies in the *beforeEach* function.

Finally, we define a test case using the *it* function and make an expectation using the *expect* function. In this case, we are expecting the component to be truthy, indicating that it has been successfully created.

6.2.5 Conclusion

Setting up Karma for your Angular projects allows you to run unit tests in real browsers, ensuring that your code works correctly across different environments. By following the steps outlined in this section, you should now have a basic understanding of how to set up Karma and write unit tests for your Angular applications.

6.3 Effective Debugging Techniques

Debugging is an essential skill for any developer, and Angular provides several powerful tools and techniques to help you identify and fix issues in your application. In this section, we will explore some effective debugging techniques that will assist you in troubleshooting and resolving problems in your Angular projects.

6.3.1 Understanding Error Messages

When encountering an error in your Angular application, the first step is to understand the error message. Angular provides detailed error messages that can give you valuable insights into the cause of the issue. Take the time to read and understand the error message, as it often contains information about the specific component, template, or service that is causing the problem.

6.3.2 Using Console Logging

Console logging is a simple yet powerful technique for debugging your Angular application. By strategically placing console.log statements in your code, you can output relevant information to the browser console and track the flow of your application. This can help you identify the values of variables, track the execution order of functions, and pinpoint the location of errors.

6.3.3 Leveraging the Angular DevTools Extension

The Angular DevTools extension is a browser extension that provides additional debugging capabilities specifically tailored for Angular applications. It allows you to inspect the component tree, view the state of your application, and monitor the performance of your Angular application. By leveraging the Angular DevTools extension, you can gain deeper insights into the inner workings of your application and identify potential issues more efficiently.

6.3.4 Using Breakpoints

Breakpoints are a powerful debugging feature available in most modern browsers. By placing breakpoints in your code, you can pause the execution of your application at specific points and inspect the state of your variables and objects. This can be particularly useful when trying to understand the flow of your application or when investigating the cause of a specific issue.

6.3.5 Debugging Template Issues

Angular templates are a critical part of your application, and debugging template-related issues can sometimes be challenging. To assist with template debugging, Angular provides a set of template debugging tools. By enabling template debugging, you can visualize the structure of your templates, highlight bindings, and identify potential issues with template syntax or data binding.

6.3.6 Using Augury for Angular Debugging

Augury is a powerful Chrome extension that provides advanced debugging capabilities for Angular applications. It allows you to inspect the component tree, view the state of your application, and analyze the performance of your Angular application. Augury also provides a detailed timeline view that helps you understand the sequence of events and identify potential performance bottlenecks.

6.3.7 Reproducing and Isolating Issues

When debugging an issue, it is crucial to be able to reproduce the problem consistently. By creating a minimal, isolated test case that reproduces the issue, you can focus your debugging efforts and eliminate any unnecessary complexity. This can involve creating a simplified version of your application or using tools like StackBlitz or CodeSandbox to create a reproducible environment.

6.3.8 Using the Angular CLI Debugger

The Angular CLI provides a built-in debugger that allows you to debug your Angular applications directly from the command line. By running your application in debug mode and attaching a debugger, you can set breakpoints, step through your code, and inspect the state of your application. This can be particularly useful when debugging complex issues or when working with server-side rendering.

6.3.9 Analyzing Network Requests

Network requests are an integral part of modern web applications, and debugging issues related to network requests can be challenging. To assist with network request debugging, Angular provides a set of tools that allow you to inspect and analyze network requests. By monitoring the network traffic, you can identify potential issues with API calls, track the response times, and analyze the data being sent and received.

6.3.10 Collaborating with Others

Debugging complex issues often requires collaboration with other developers or team members. By leveraging tools like screen sharing, remote debugging, or code review platforms, you can effectively collaborate with others to identify and resolve issues. Additionally, documenting your debugging process and sharing your findings with others can help build a knowledge base and facilitate future debugging efforts.

By mastering these effective debugging techniques, you will be well-equipped to tackle any issues that arise during the development of your Angular applications. Remember, debugging is a skill that improves with practice, so don't be discouraged if you encounter challenges along the way. With time and experience, you will become a proficient debugger and be able to resolve issues efficiently.

7 Deployment and Best Practices

7.1 Deploying Angular Applications

Once you have built your Angular application, the next step is to deploy it so that it can be accessed by users. Deploying an Angular application involves preparing your code for production, optimizing its performance, and hosting it on a server. In this section, we will explore the different steps involved in deploying an Angular application and discuss some best practices to follow.

7.1.1 Preparing for Production

Before deploying your Angular application, it is important to optimize it for production. This involves several steps to ensure that your application runs efficiently and performs well.

7.1.1.1 AOT Compilation

Ahead-of-Time (AOT) compilation is a process that converts your Angular application's TypeScript code into optimized JavaScript code during the build process. AOT compilation improves the performance of your application by reducing the size of the bundle and eliminating the need for the browser to compile the code at runtime. To enable AOT compilation, you can use the --*aot* flag when running the build command.

7.1.1.2 Tree Shaking

Tree shaking is a technique used to eliminate unused code from your application's bundle. It analyzes your code and removes any modules or functions that are not being used, resulting in a smaller bundle size. To enable tree shaking, make sure that your application is using the ES2015 module syntax and that you have enabled the --*prod* flag when running the build command.

7.1.1.3 Production Mode

Enabling production mode in your Angular application provides additional performance optimizations. It disables certain development features and enables more aggressive optimizations, resulting in a faster and smaller bundle. To enable production mode, set the *production* property to *true* in the *environment.ts* file.

7.1.2 Building and Packaging

Once you have prepared your Angular application for production, the next step is to build and package it for deployment. The Angular CLI provides a convenient way to build your application and create a production-ready bundle.

To build your application, run the following command:

```
ng build --prod
```

This command will compile your application, optimize it for production, and generate a bundle in the *dist* folder. The generated bundle will contain all the necessary files, including the HTML, CSS, JavaScript, and assets required to run your application.

7.1.3 Hosting Options

After building your Angular application, you need to choose a hosting option to make it accessible to users. There are several hosting options available, depending on your requirements and budget.

7.1.3.1 Shared Hosting

Shared hosting is a cost-effective option for hosting small to medium-sized Angular applications. With shared hosting, your application shares server resources with other websites. This option is suitable for applications with low to moderate traffic and does not require advanced server configurations.

7.1.3.2 Virtual Private Server (VPS)

A Virtual Private Server (VPS) provides dedicated resources for your Angular application. It offers more control and flexibility compared to shared hosting. With a VPS, you can configure the server environment to meet your specific requirements. This option is suitable for applications with moderate to high traffic or those that require custom server configurations.

7.1.3.3 Cloud Hosting

Cloud hosting platforms, such as Amazon Web Services (AWS) and Google Cloud Platform (GCP), provide scalable and reliable hosting solutions for Angular applications. These platforms offer a wide range of services, including virtual machines, containers, and serverless computing. Cloud hosting is suitable for applications with high traffic or those that require auto-scaling and high availability.

7.1.4 Continuous Integration and Deployment

To streamline the deployment process and ensure the quality of your Angular application, consider implementing a Continuous Integration and Deployment (CI/CD) pipeline. CI/CD allows you to automate the build, testing, and deployment of your application whenever changes are made to the codebase.

Popular CI/CD tools, such as Jenkins, Travis CI, and CircleCI, can be integrated with your version control system to trigger the build and deployment process automatically. These tools can run tests, build the application, and deploy it to the hosting environment, ensuring that your application is always up to date and in a working state.

7.1.5 Monitoring and Error Tracking

Once your Angular application is deployed, it is important to monitor its performance and track any errors that occur. Monitoring tools, such as Google Analytics or New Relic, can provide insights into user behavior, page load times, and other performance metrics. Error tracking tools, such as Sentry or Rollbar, can help identify and track errors in your application, allowing you to quickly resolve issues and improve the user experience.

7.1.6 Best Practices

When deploying Angular applications, it is important to follow best practices to ensure a smooth and efficient deployment process. Here are some best practices to consider:

- Use version control to manage your codebase and track changes.

- Automate the build and deployment process using CI/CD tools.

- Regularly update dependencies to ensure your application is using the latest versions of libraries and frameworks.

- Implement caching and compression techniques to improve performance.

- Monitor your application's performance and track errors to identify and resolve issues quickly.

- Implement security measures, such as HTTPS and secure authentication, to protect your application and user data.

By following these best practices, you can ensure that your Angular application is deployed successfully and performs optimally in a production environment.

7.1.7 Conclusion

Deploying an Angular application involves preparing your code for production, building and packaging it, choosing a hosting option, and implementing monitoring and error tracking. By following best practices and using tools like CI/CD, you can streamline the deployment process and ensure a smooth and efficient deployment of your Angular application.

7.2 Code Quality and Best Practices

In this section, we will explore various code quality practices and best practices that can help you write clean, maintainable, and efficient Angular code. Following these practices will not only improve the readability of your code but also make it easier to debug, test, and maintain.

7.2.1 Consistent Coding Style

Maintaining a consistent coding style throughout your Angular project is crucial for readability and collaboration. It is recommended to follow the official Angular Style Guide, which provides a set of conventions and guidelines for writing Angular code. This guide covers topics such as naming conventions, file organization, component structure, and more. Adhering to a consistent coding style will make your codebase more cohesive and easier to understand for both you and your team members.

7.2.2 Modular Architecture

Angular encourages a modular architecture, where you break your application into smaller, reusable modules. Each module should have a specific responsibility and should be independent of other modules. This modular approach promotes code reusability, maintainability, and testability. When designing your modules, consider the Single Responsibility Principle (SRP) and keep them focused on a specific feature or functionality. This will make it easier to understand and modify individual modules without affecting the entire application.

7.2.3 Use TypeScript Features

TypeScript is the recommended language for building Angular applications. It brings static typing and additional features to JavaScript, making your code more robust and less prone to errors. Take advantage of TypeScript features such as type annotations, interfaces, and enums to provide better type safety and improve code readability. Utilize features like classes, modules, and decorators to organize your code and leverage the power of object-oriented programming.

7.2.4 Error Handling and Logging

Proper error handling and logging are essential for identifying and resolving issues in your Angular application. Use Angular's error handling mechanisms, such as the ErrorHandler class, to catch and handle errors in a centralized manner. Implement logging mechanisms, such as the console.log() function or a dedicated logging library, to log relevant information during development and production. This will help you track down issues, debug your application, and provide valuable insights for troubleshooting.

7.2.5 Performance Optimization

Optimizing the performance of your Angular application is crucial for delivering a smooth user experience. Consider the following best practices to improve performance:

- Minimize the use of two-way data binding, as it can impact performance. Prefer one-way data binding whenever possible.

- Use Angular's ChangeDetectionStrategy.OnPush strategy for components that don't require frequent updates. This reduces unnecessary change detection cycles.

- Implement lazy loading for modules and routes to load only the necessary code when needed, reducing the initial load time.

- Use trackBy function in ngFor loops to improve rendering performance when working with lists.

- Optimize the size of your application by enabling production mode, tree shaking, and code minification.

7.2.6 Testing Best Practices

Writing tests for your Angular application is crucial to ensure its correctness and maintainability. Follow these best practices to write effective tests:

- Write unit tests for individual components, services, and other Angular constructs to verify their behavior in isolation.

- Use mocking and stubbing techniques to isolate dependencies and focus on testing the specific functionality of the unit under test.

- Utilize Angular's testing utilities, such as TestBed and ComponentFixture, to create and interact with components during testing.

- Write integration tests to verify the interaction between different components and services.

- Use code coverage tools to measure the effectiveness of your tests and ensure that critical parts of your codebase are adequately covered.

7.2.7 Continuous Integration and Deployment

Implementing a continuous integration (CI) and deployment (CD) pipeline for your Angular application can streamline the development process and ensure the quality of your code. Use popular CI/CD tools like Jenkins, Travis CI, or GitLab CI/CD to automate tasks such as building, testing, and deploying your application. Set up automated tests to run on every code commit and trigger deployments to staging or production environments. This will help catch issues early and ensure that only stable and tested code is deployed.

7.2.8 Documentation and Code Comments

Documenting your code and providing clear comments is essential for improving code maintainability and facilitating collaboration. Use tools like JSDoc or TypeScript annotations to generate API documentation for your components, services, and modules. Write descriptive comments to explain complex logic, assumptions, or any non-obvious code behavior. Documenting your code will make it easier for other developers to understand and work with your codebase.

Following these code quality practices and best practices will help you build robust, maintainable, and efficient Angular applications. By writing clean and well-structured code, you can enhance the readability, testability, and maintainability of your projects.

8 Glossary

8.1 Technical Terms and Definitions

In this chapter, we will provide a comprehensive glossary of technical terms and definitions used throughout this book. It is important to have a clear understanding of these terms as they are fundamental to working with Angular and building dynamic web applications.

8.1.1 Angular

Angular is a popular open-source framework for building web applications. It is developed and maintained by Google and provides a comprehensive set of tools and features for building dynamic, responsive applications.

8.1.2 Component

A component is a fundamental building block of an Angular application. It is a self-contained unit that encapsulates the HTML template, CSS styles, and the logic required to render a specific part of the user interface.

8.1.3 Module

A module is a container for a group of related components, directives, services, and other code. It provides a way to organize and manage the different parts of an Angular application.

8.1.4 Service

A service is a reusable piece of code that provides specific functionality to different parts of an application. It is typically used to encapsulate business logic, data access, or other common tasks.

8.1.5 Data Binding

Data binding is a mechanism in Angular that allows you to establish a connection between the data in your application and the user interface. It enables you to keep the UI in sync with the underlying data and provides a way to handle user input and update the data accordingly.

8.1.6 Dependency Injection

Dependency injection is a design pattern used in Angular to manage the dependencies between different parts of an application. It allows you to define the dependencies of a component or service and have them automatically injected by the Angular framework.

8.1.7 Routing

Routing is the process of navigating between different views or pages in a single-page application. In Angular, the routing module provides a way to define the routes and handle the navigation between them.

8.1.8 Reactive Programming

Reactive programming is a programming paradigm that focuses on asynchronous data streams and the propagation of changes. In Angular, reactive programming is often used with the RxJS library to handle events, manage state, and perform complex data transformations.

8.1.9 NgRx

NgRx is a state management library for Angular applications. It is based on the principles of Redux and provides a way to manage the state of an application in a predictable and centralized manner.

8.1.10 Performance Optimization

Performance optimization refers to the process of improving the speed and efficiency of an application. In the context of Angular, it involves techniques such as lazy loading, code splitting, and optimizing the rendering and data flow to ensure a smooth and responsive user experience.

8.1.11 Unit Testing

Unit testing is a software testing technique where individual units of code are tested in isolation to ensure that they function correctly. In Angular, unit tests are typically written using the Jasmine testing framework and executed using the Karma test runner.

8.1.12 Debugging

Debugging is the process of identifying and fixing errors or issues in a software application. In Angular, effective debugging techniques involve using tools such as the browser's developer console, breakpoints, and logging to track down and resolve issues.

8.1.13 Deployment

Deployment refers to the process of making an application available for use. In the context of Angular, it involves preparing the application for production, optimizing the code, and deploying it to a web server or a cloud platform.

8.1.14 Code Quality

Code quality refers to the overall quality and maintainability of the codebase. It involves following best practices, writing clean and readable code, and using tools and techniques to ensure that the code is free from bugs and easy to understand and maintain.

8.1.15 Best Practices

Best practices are a set of guidelines and recommendations that are considered to be the most effective and efficient way of doing something. In the context of Angular, following best practices helps to ensure that the application is well-structured, performant, and maintainable.

This glossary provides a brief overview of the key technical terms and definitions used throughout this book. It is recommended to refer back to this chapter whenever you come across a term that you are unfamiliar with or need clarification on. Having a solid understanding of these terms will greatly enhance your ability to work with Angular and build dynamic web applications.

www.ingramcontent.com/pod-product-compliance
Lightning Source LLC
LaVergne TN
LVHW051742050326
832903LV00029B/2666